BLACK HOLES

ENERGY

GALAXIES

GRAVITY

LIGHT

MYSTERIES OF THE UNIVERSE

MASS & MATTER

SPACE & TIME

STARS

MYSTERIES OF
THE UNIVERSE

Space & Time

JIM WHITING

CREATIVE EDUCATION

Published by Creative Education

P.O. Box 227, Mankato, Minnesota 56002

Creative Education is an imprint of The Creative Company

www.thecreativecompany.us

Design and production by Blue Design

Art direction by Rita Marshall

Printed in the United States of America

Photographs by Getty Images (Apic, Andreas Cellarius, DEA PICTURE
LIBRARY/De Agostini, Tony Hallas, Ivan Petrovich Keler-Viliandi, NASA/
Time & Life Pictures, Jean-Luc PETIT/Gamma-Rapho, SSPL, STRINGER/
AFP, Universal History Archive, Bruno Vincent, Warner Bros.), iStockphoto
(Evgeny Terentev), NASA (NASA, NASA/ESA/F. Paresce [INAF-IASF,
Bologna, Italy]/R. O'Connell [University of Virginia, Charlottesville]/Wide
Field Camera 3 Science Oversight Committee, NASA/STScl/Magellan/U.
Arizona/D. Clowe et al.)

Cover and folio illustration © 2011 Alex Ryan

Library of Congress Cataloging-in-Publication Data

Whiting, Jim.

Space and time / by Jim Whiting.

p. cm. — (Mysteries of the universe)

Includes bibliographical references and index.

Summary: An examination of the science behind the abstract and physical
concepts of space and time, including relevant theories and history-
making discoveries as well as topics of current and future research.

ISBN 978-1-60818-192-6

1. Space and time—Juvenile literature. 2. Relativity (Physics)—Juvenile
literature. I. Title.

QC173.59.S65W45 2012

530.11—dc23   2011040146

CPSIA: 021413 PO1656

9 8 7 6 5 4 3 2

An English reflecting telescope of the 1930s

TABLE OF CONTENTS

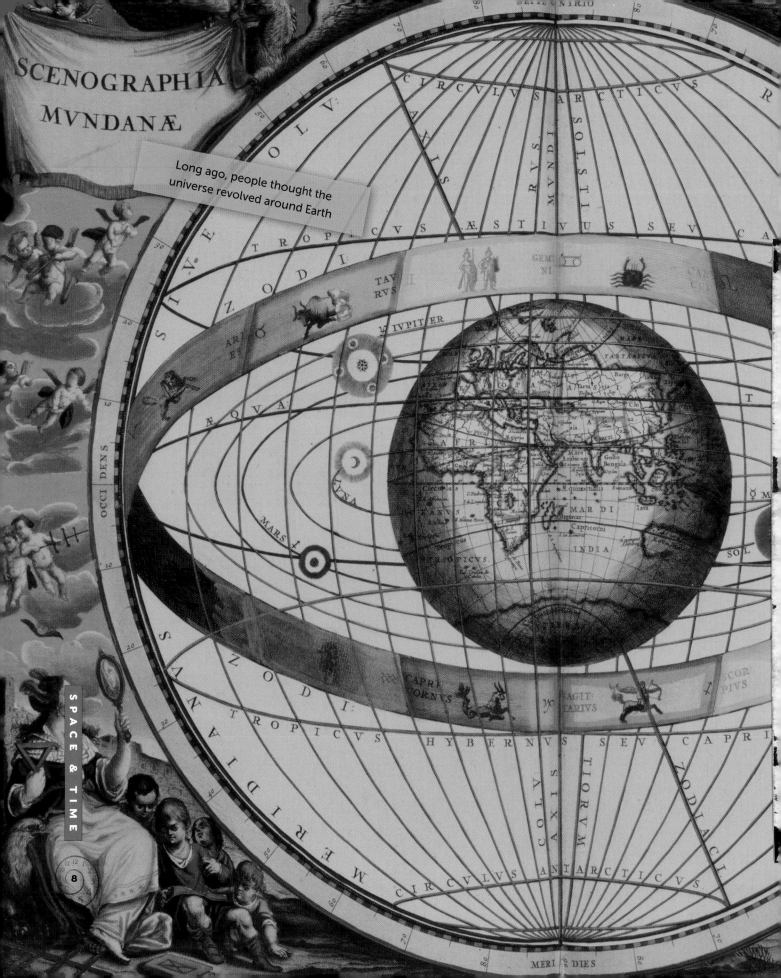

Long ago, people thought the universe revolved around Earth

INTRODUCTION

For most of human history, the true nature of the universe was shrouded in myth and mystery. About 400 years ago, scientists began unraveling those mysteries. Their efforts were so successful that American **physicist** Albert Michelson wrote in 1894, "The more important fundamental laws and facts of physical science have all been discovered, and these are now so firmly established that the possibility of their ever being supplemented in consequence of new discoveries is exceedingly remote." William Thomson, Baron Kelvin, perhaps that era's most famous physicist, echoed Michelson: "There is nothing new to be discovered in physics now. All that remains is more and more precise measurement." Both men were wrong. Within a few years, scientists had revealed the makeup of the tiny **atom** and the unexpected vastness of outer space. Yet the universe doesn't yield its mysteries easily, and much remains to be discovered.

At any given moment in time, a person or an object occupies a certain point in space. This seems obvious. But all may not be as it seems. There are many deep questions about space and time that remain to be answered. What is space, really? How far does it extend? Is space expanding, contracting, or static? Did space have a beginning? We can ask some of the same questions about time. Was there a time before time? Will time eventually come to an end? How do we tell time? For as much as we already know about space and time, there seems to be equally as much that we have yet to grasp.

Baron Kelvin taught at Scotland's University of Glasgow for 53 years

FIGURING OUT WHERE WE ARE

"All the world's a stage," wrote English playwright William Shakespeare more than 400 years ago, "and all the men and women merely players. They have their exits and their entrances." We might think of space as the stage and time as the exits and entrances. Time provides the framework of our lives, a fact that the author of the biblical book of Ecclesiastes knew well: "To every thing there is a season, and a time to every purpose under the heaven." There is a time for birth and a time for death. A time for hurting and healing. Giving and taking. Being silent and speaking up. Loving and hating. War and peace.

We rely on time to construct our daily lives. We get up at a certain time. We have to be at school at a certain time, and we go home when the final bell rings. We eat dinner, then do homework and perhaps watch our favorite TV shows, which all come on at certain times. Many sports events depend on time, too. A "buzzer-beater" is a last-second shot that wins a basketball game as time expires. Track runners try to beat their previous best times. Even though baseball games don't have clocks, they usually last for nine innings—also a measure of time.

Keeping up with time is easy nowadays. Many of us have wristwatches or cell phones and computers that display the current time. There are clocks inside and outside public and private buildings. Our ancestors would have envied us. This readily accessible knowledge of accurate time is a recent development, especially with the degree of certainty we have.

Clocks aren't the only method of telling time. People also use calendars to mark the passage of days, weeks, months, and years. While there are many different calendars based on custom and culture, the one most commonly used today counts the years based on when Jesus Christ was supposed to have been born. The term B.C. stands for "before Christ," while A.D. stands for the Latin phrase anno Domini, "in the year of

Outer space is a vast stage for exploration

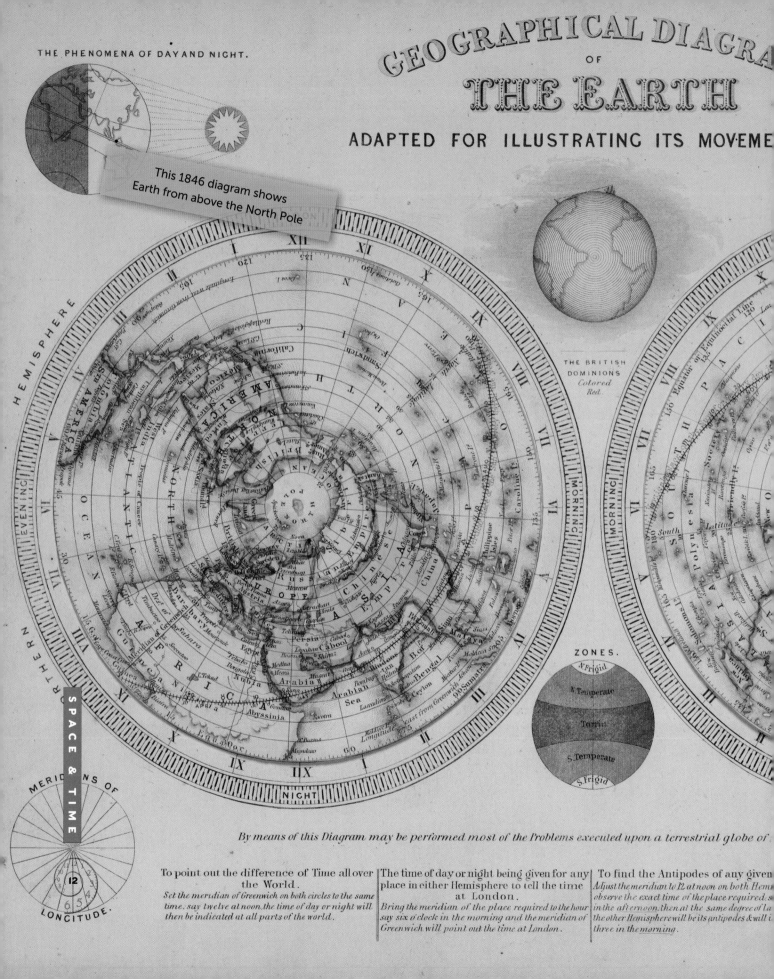

THE PHENOMENA OF DAY AND NIGHT.

GEOGRAPHICAL DIAGRA
OF
THE EARTH
ADAPTED FOR ILLUSTRATING ITS MOVEME

This 1846 diagram shows Earth from above the North Pole

THE BRITISH DOMINIONS
Colored Red.

ZONES.

N. Frigid
N. Temperate
Torrid
S. Temperate
S. Frigid

NIGHT

MERIDIANS OF
LONGITUDE.

SPACE & TIME

By means of this Diagram may be performed most of the Problems executed upon a terrestrial globe of

To point out the difference of Time all over the World.
Set the meridian of Greenwich on both circles to the same time, say twelve at noon, the time of day or night will then be indicated at all parts of the world.

The time of day or night being given for any place in either Hemisphere to tell the time at London.
Bring the meridian of the place required to the hour say six o'clock in the morning and the meridian of Greenwich will point out the time at London.

To find the Antipodes of any given
Adjust the meridian to 12 at noon on both Hem observe the exact time of the place required in the afternoon, then at the same degree of la the other Hemisphere will be its antipodes & will three in the morning.

the Lord." Although many scholars believe Christ was actually born about 4 B.C., the reasoning still stands. This calendar is based on a solar year of about 365.25 days.

Although we can't measure it in the same way as calendars and clocks enable us to keep time, we know that we are also grounded in space. Many people think of "space" as outer space, the universe that lies beyond Earth. But "space" also refers to the three dimensions of our location at any given moment: the length, width, and height we occupy. A famous line from American playwright Thornton Wilder's classic work *Our Town* refers to a letter a minister sends to one of his young parishioners when she is ill. The minister addresses the letter to "Jane Crofut; The Crofut Farm; Grover's Corners; Sutton County; New Hampshire; United States of America; Continent of North America; Western Hemisphere; the Earth; the Solar System; the Universe; the Mind of God." Starting with Jane's name and specific location, the minister broadens the definition of "address" to include every region of space of which she is a part.

We can further define where we are on Earth by using latitude and longitude. Latitude measures the distance north and south of the equator, while longitude measures distance east and west of the prime meridian (a line that passes through Greenwich, England, and divides the earth into Eastern and Western Hemispheres). Both latitude and longitude are expressed in degrees. Each degree in turn is divided into 60 minutes and each minute into 60 seconds.

Lines of latitude lie parallel to the equator and encircle the earth. Latitude is expressed as north latitude (north of the equator) and south latitude (south of the equator). The equator is at 0°, while the North Pole is 90° N, and the South Pole is 90° S. Each degree of latitude, whether north or south, is equal to a distance of about 69 miles (111 km).

Lines of longitude, also known as meridians, start and finish at the poles. According to an international agreement made in 1884, time is based on the mean solar time at 0° longitude, or the prime meridian at the Royal Observatory in Greenwich. When it

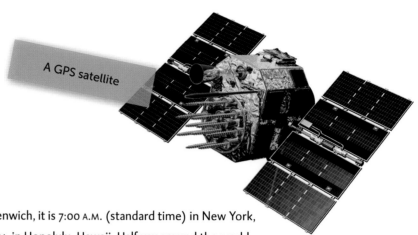

A GPS satellite

is noon Universal Time (UT) at Greenwich, it is 7:00 A.M. (standard time) in New York, 4:00 A.M. in Los Angeles, and 2:00 A.M. in Honolulu, Hawaii. Halfway around the world from London, at the **International Date Line**, a new day has begun.

To determine longitude, the Earth is divided into 360 degrees, starting at Greenwich. Moving west to the International Date Line is west longitude, while the other direction is east longitude. Each degree of longitude is about 69 miles (111 km) at the equator, diminishing to 49 miles (79 km) at 45° N or 45° S (halfway to the poles) and ending at nothing at the poles.

We can determine any point on Earth by the intersection of latitude and longitude. For example, the White House in Washington, D.C. is located at 38°53'52" N and 77°2'13" W. Today, a network of 24 Global Positioning System (GPS) satellites in Earth **orbit** gives us this information in a fraction of a second, pinpointing locations to within a few yards. GPS began as a military project, though in the 1980s it was expanded for civilian use.

People use a different designation to measure the immense distances between Earth and points in outer space. To avoid working with huge numbers in determining those distances, **astronomers** use a measurement called light years. Light travels at the speed of 186,282 miles (299,792 km) per second, covering nearly 6 trillion miles (9.5 trillion km) per year. That distance represents one light year. So instead of writing that the nearest star to Earth (other than the sun), Proxima Centauri, is about 24 trillion miles (40 trillion km) away, we say it is about 4.2 light years away.

There is one fundamental difference between space and time. We can, and often do, revisit the same point in space, but we can't do the same with time. In the previous example from *Our Town*, Jane Crofut almost certainly wakes up nearly every morning in her bed at her family's farm. She probably also goes to the same school every day during the week, plays with the same friends in the same places, and sits down with her family for meals at the same table. In other words, in space, she can do the same things over and over again.

St. Augustine (354–430) lived in what is now Algeria

We can't "do" time over and over again, though. In a way, time is similar to a flowing river, always carrying us downstream. It is a succession of present moments, which quickly become our past. We can look forward to the future, but it then becomes the present for an instant and then the past as well. As one dictionary puts it, time is "a **nonspatial continuum** in which events occur in apparently irreversible succession from the past through the present to the future." Past, present, and future we can all understand. But what about those other concepts mentioned in the dictionary definition? More than 16 centuries ago, the early Christian philosopher St. Augustine threw up his hands in despair, exclaiming, "What then is time? If no one asks me, I know what it is. If I wish to explain it to him who asks, I do not know." We may have an **intuitive** understanding of what time is, but it's hard to put it into words.

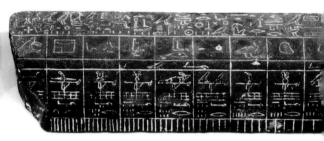

Wooden and stone cubit rods from Egypt

DEFINING TIME AND SPACE

As people began settling down into established communities, perhaps as early as 10,000 years ago, measuring space and time became important. The first recorded unit of measurement of space was the cubit, which arose in Egypt and Sumer about 4,500 years ago and was roughly equivalent to the length of a person's forearm. The Greeks used the *stade*, about 200 yards (183 m) long, as their unit of measurement. The Olympics and other Greek athletic events used the stade as the standard competitive distance, and it became the origin of our word "stadium."

From the Romans came the term "mile." The Latin word *mille* means "thousand," and a Roman mile represented 1,000 double paces (one step with each foot). This came out to a little less than 5,000 feet (about 1,500 m). The English later adopted the mile, though they continued to use other measurements as well: the foot, the rod, and the furlong (derived from "furrow length," or how far a team of oxen could drag a plow before needing to rest). The rod was established as 16.5 feet (5.03 m), and the furlong became fixed as 40 rods, or 660 feet (201.2 m). In 1592, the English government established a law that said the mile was 8 furlongs, or a total of 5,280 feet (1,609 m).

In the aftermath of the French Revolution (which began in 1789), the French wanted a new unit of measurement to go along with the other societal changes they had made. They called this unit the meter, derived from the Greek word *metron*, or "a measure." It would be one ten-millionth of the length of the arc from the equator to the North Pole. While acceptance of the metric system was initially slow, by the late 1800s, it was in common use throughout Europe. In 1983, the meter was redefined as the distance that light travels in a **vacuum** in 1/299,792,458 of a second. Either way, a meter is equal to 39.37 inches.

When early humans roamed the earth in search of food, they thought of two basic times. One was daytime, the period between the rising and setting of the sun. The other was nighttime, when the sun was gone, and the only light came from the moon and stars. With the rise of civilizations that depended on agriculture, people needed a more accurate system for telling time and knowing when to plant and harvest crops.

A ncient peoples began studying the phases of the moon and eventually discovered that a complete cycle from new moon to new moon took 29 and a half days. More than 6,000 years ago, Egyptian calendars based on these **lunar** cycles designated three seasons: flood time (based on the annual overflowing of the Nile River, which deposited nutrients that allowed crops to grow in the otherwise dry land), seed time, and harvest time. Around

Plan *of the* Instrument.

A 1790s theodolite to measure horizontal and vertical angles in surveying

Mathematician Christopher Clavius came up with the Gregorian calendar

When Julius Caesar was appointed permanent dictator of Rome in 46 B.C., the calendar was a mess. For centuries, it had been based on the lunar cycle. To align it with the solar calendar of 365.25 days used by the Egyptians, an extra month would periodically be added. Because of continual political turmoil in Rome, that addition had been neglected for many years. Now the calendar was three months off. Caesar added three temporary months between November and December in 46 B.C., giving that year 445 days. What became known as the Julian calendar began the following year, 45 B.C., with 3 years of 365 days followed by 366 days every fourth year. The month of Quintilis (Caesar's birth month) was renamed July to honor him, and Sextilis became August for Emperor Augustus. To make August the same length as July—31 days—a day was removed from February. The Julian calendar was off by about 11 minutes every year. By the late 1500s, the discrepancy had grown to 10 days, forcing Pope Gregory XIII to cut 10 days from October 1582, based on mathematical recommendations. The Pope also specified that years divisible by 100 would be made leap years only if they were also divisible by 400. This is the Gregorian calendar, the one we use today.

2000 B.C., calendars in **Babylon** featured months that lasted 29 or 30 days.

The lunar month is based on the amount of time it takes the moon to complete an orbit of Earth. It bears no relationship to the solar year, which is based on how long it takes Earth to orbit the sun (about 365 days). To make up for the inconsistency between the two, some calendars simply added an extra month every few years.

Lunar and solar cycles are based on natural phenomena. Other time divisions, such as the week, are man-made. During their observations of the heavens, ancient observers noted that the sun, the moon, and the thousands of stars they could see followed regular and predictable paths. There were five that didn't. The Greeks called them *planetai*, meaning "wandering," which eventually became our word "planet." Along with the sun and the moon, the ancients regarded those five planets known at the time—Mercury,

The Greek concept of a varying, seasonal "hour" came from sundials

Venus, Mars, Jupiter, and Saturn—as having special powers and honored each one with its own day. This seems to be the foundation of our seven-day week.

D ays were soon divided into hours. The Egyptians identified several stars that appeared at regular intervals during the night. They used those intervals to divide the night into 12 equal parts. Later, they adapted the same plan for the day, giving us 24 hours. The Babylonians went even further, dividing the hour into 60 minutes and each minute into 60 seconds. The Greeks and Romans adopted similar systems, and the English word "hour" comes from the Greek word for "limited time" or "season."

The ancients used static, or immobile, devices such as sundials to keep track of the passage of time. The first mechanical timekeeping devices appeared in Europe around A.D. 1300. A weight attached to a system of gears slowly descended, causing the gears to drive a single hand around a circular face divided into 12 equal parts. At each hour, a hammer struck a bell. The medieval Latin word for bell is *clocca*, which became our word "clock."

Increasingly accurate means of timekeeping were invented in the successive centuries. The climax came near the end of the 20th century with the invention of the atomic clock. A second on an atomic clock consists of 9,192,631,770 vibrations of an atom of cesium, an **alkali metal** that is 1 of just 3 metals found in a liquid state at room temperature. This measurement is so accurate that it loses just a single second in 20 million years.

Although time was being measured with increasing accuracy, no one knew when time had begun. In the 1600s, Irish priest James Ussher traced the chronology of the Bible and concluded that Earth had been created in 4004 B.C. Starting in the late 1700s, people who examined fossils began realizing that Earth was at least hundreds of millions of years old. This revelation was startling on many levels, not the least of which was the thought that, if Earth was that old, the sun had to be even older. But no one had any idea how the sun could have burned for so long.

This mystery was finally solved in the 1920s. Astronomers realized that the sun—and every other star—was composed largely of a chemical **element** called hydrogen. Through a process called fusion, two hydrogen atoms fuse, or come together, to form a new element called deuterium, or heavy hydrogen. Two of these newly formed deuterium atoms in turn fuse to form a helium atom. During this process—which occurs in a fraction of a second—a tiny amount of matter is transformed into energy. A star's seemingly endless supply of hydrogen atoms allows it to continue this process for billions and billions of years.

The Prague Astronomical Clock (Czech Republic) has kept time since 1410

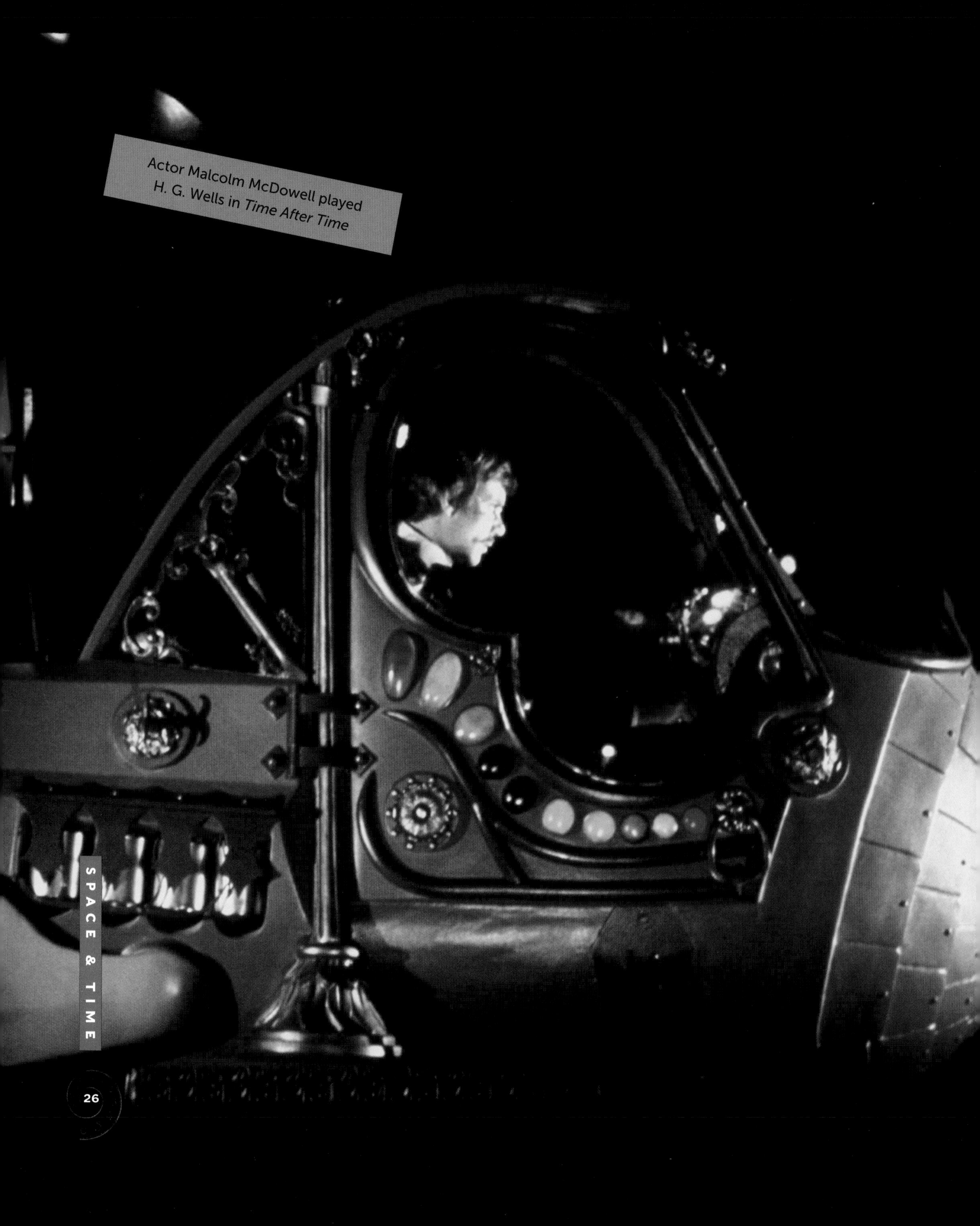

Actor Malcolm McDowell played H. G. Wells in *Time After Time*

The First Time Travelers

In the 19th century, writers began thinking about going back and forth in time. American author Washington Irving's character Rip Van Winkle goes to sleep one afternoon and wakes up 20 years later. American author Mark Twain's *A Connecticut Yankee in King Arthur's Court* (published in 1889) takes its American hero back to the age of King Arthur and the Knights of the Round Table. Probably the best-known book in this field is British author H. G. Wells's novel *The Time Machine*. In it, a man known only as the Time Traveller invents a time machine. First, he travels to the year 802,701, where humans live peacefully but do little work. His journeys farther into the future show the decline of Earth. The novel later inspired several movies. One is *Time After Time* (1979), which begins in 1893 when Wells himself invents a time machine. Jack the Ripper uses it to flee to San Francisco, California, in 1979 and begin another killing spree. Wells pursues him and meets a woman who nearly becomes a victim. He saves her, sends Jack far into the future with no hope of ever returning, then goes back to 1893 with the woman who has now become his wife.

The 20th century brought about a revolution in thinking about the relationship between space and time as well. The three dimensions of space—length, width, and height—merged with time to create a four-dimensional **entity** called spacetime. Equally fundamentally, the notion that space and time were unchanging and eternal had itself begun to change. In the late 1920s, Belgian priest and astronomer Georges Lemaître developed a theory he called the "primeval atom" to account for the beginning of space and time (renamed the Big Bang theory in 1949). According to this theory, about 13.7 billion years ago, the universe was in an extremely hot, dense, and compacted state. It began to expand almost instantaneously. As scientists have studied this expansion, they have turned up even more mysteries.

Galileo's powers of observation led him to many discoveries

UNRAVELING THE MYSTERIES

One of the earliest—and certainly one of the most enduring—efforts to measure time and space came from the ancient Greek mathematician Euclid (c. 325–270 B.C.). His book *The Elements* set out the principles of Euclidean **geometry** and became the world's most important mathematics textbook for 2,000 years. A key element in Euclidean geometry is that the sum of the angles of a triangle is 180 degrees. Using this knowledge, ancient surveyors—and modern ones, too—conducted accurate surveys of land and property without knowing all the measurements of the area they were surveying. For example, knowing the length of one side of the triangle and the angles on each end makes it possible to figure out the other measurements.

Timekeeping took much longer to acquire the same precision, as even mechanical clocks were often inaccurate. Italian scientist Galileo Galilei (1564–1642) laid the groundwork for greater accuracy when he observed the motion of a lamp suspended from the ceiling of a cathedral as it swung back and forth. Using his pulse to keep time, he noticed that, no matter how large or small the arc of the lamp, it always took the same amount of time to return to its original position. This observation convinced him that a **pendulum clock** would be more precise and use smaller increments, or divisions, than a mechanical clock. Galileo sketched out a plan for a clock driven by a pendulum but never made one. In 1656, Dutch mathematician and astronomer Christiaan Huygens (1629–95) constructed the first working pendulum clock.

English physicist and mathematician Isaac Newton (1643–1727) carried Galileo's ideas even further. Newton believed that everything in the universe was under the control of unvarying physical laws, such as the law of **gravity**. Space went on and on, and so did time. In his groundbreaking 1687 book *Philosophiae Naturalis Principia Mathematica* (better known simply as the *Principia*), he wrote, "Absolute space, in its own nature,… remains always similar and immovable…. Absolute, true and mathematical time, of itself, and from its own nature, flows **equably** without relation to anything external." In other words, space and time are independent of each other, and they can't be compressed or expanded.

Eventually, physicists would question this belief. One of the first steps came in the early 1800s, with the work of German mathematician Karl Gauss (1777–1855). In an 1824 letter to fellow mathematician Ferdinand Karl Schweikart, Gauss wrote, "I have therefore from time to time in jest expressed the desire that Euclidean geometry would not be correct." Although he was reluctant to publish any of his ideas refuting Euclid's and Newton's worldviews, Gauss was almost certainly the first person to develop the idea of non-Euclidean geometry. Because Euclidean geometry is based on the idea of flat surfaces, when the curvature of Earth is taken into account, Euclidean geometry may not work anymore. For example, on a flat map the shortest distance between New York City and London, England, is a straight line connecting the two cities. But on Earth's actual surface, the shortest distance is a great circle that passes over eastern Canada and goes as far north as the southern tip of Greenland. Airlines today take advantage of this knowledge to save both time and fuel.

Gauss's student Bernhard Riemann (1826–66) further developed his teacher's ideas. He showed that this new geometry could apply to any curved surface in three or even more dimensions. For example, lines of longitude at the equator form right angles. But when those lines are carried all the way to the North or South Pole, without having changed at all, they meet to form a triangle. Because both of the lines at the equator are right angles, totaling 180 degrees, the addition of the angle at the pole makes the sum greater than 180.

German-born physicist Albert Einstein (1879–1955) took advantage of the work of Gauss and Riemann to help develop his groundbreaking theories of relativity. He

This type of surveying instrument
was used to find the length of a meter

31

Sailing was a favorite pastime of Einstein's

began in 1905 with the special theory of relativity. According to this theory, space and time aren't the absolutes Newton had said they were. Instead, they are relative to the state of motion of whoever is observing them. What is constant is the speed of light. Einstein realized that the closer a person came to approaching the speed of light, the more time would slow down. For example, if there were twin brothers, and one twin remained on Earth while the other took a space voyage at nearly the speed of light, the space-traveling twin would actually be younger than his sibling when he returned. Time would have slowed down for him without his knowledge, since his watch would have kept the same time as on Earth.

Many people had difficulty understanding Einstein's theory. To help explain it, he jokingly said, "Put your hand on a hot stove for a minute, and it seems like an hour. Sit with a pretty girl for an hour, and it seems like a minute. That's relativity." On a more serious level, he incorporated gravity into the special theory and came up with the general theory of relativity 10 years later. He acknowledged the role of his predecessors, saying, "This theory of surfaces by Gauss has been extended by Riemann to continua of any arbitrary number of dimensions and has thus paved the way for the general theory of relativity." According to the general theory, space and time are linked in a four-dimensional, curved construction called spacetime that also accounts for the pull of gravity. To illustrate this, think about what would happen if you put a bowling ball in the center of a trampoline, then put a marble at the edge of the trampoline. The marble would begin rolling in a straight line before being attracted to the dent created by the bowling ball and circling the ball. In the same way, Earth circles the sun.

Everything in spacetime follows a curved path. If a person goes to a firing range and shoots a pistol, the bullet flies seemingly straight ahead and imbeds itself in the target a fraction of a second later. If that same person throws a ball, it follows along a curve and takes longer to reach the target. But if the time dimension is accounted for, the bullet is shown to follow a curving path as well. This seemingly impossible concept is, according to Einstein—and proven by many physicists after him—entirely correct.

Even as late as Einstein's era, astronomers had no idea of the immense size of the universe. Most believed it consisted of a single **galaxy**, our own Milky Way. Starting in the 1920s, American astronomer Edwin Hubble (1889–1953) began to make a series of startling findings. One was that there were many more galaxies than the Milky Way, and another was that the universe was continuing to expand in all directions. The situation was similar to what happens to a balloon with dots on it as air is pumped into it. As the balloon continues to expand, the dots (representing galaxies in this case) move away from each other on the balloon's surface. In less than a century after Hubble's observations, astronomers—some while using a space telescope named for him—would establish that the number of galaxies was truly mind-boggling.

Meteor showers come from comets within the Milky Way

Europe's GNSS, nicknamed Galileo, is expected to begin service in 2014

THE FUTURE (AND PAST) OF SPACETIME

Research into the nature of space and time continues. Some of it comes from the Centre for Quantum Engineering and Space-Time Research (QUEST). Founded in 2007, the group is organized around Germany's Leibniz Universitat Hannover and four other German institutions. More than 200 scientists are directly involved in ongoing QUEST research. QUEST specializes in the production of high-precision clocks, especially for possible use in future space missions. It also works to enhance some countries' global navigation satellite systems (GNSS), which provide instantaneous information about where a person or object is located and measure the gravitational field of Earth.

Perhaps the biggest remaining mystery in the realm of space and time is the ultimate fate of the universe. There are basically three possibilities. First, although the universe is still expanding, the rate of this expansion has begun to decrease because of the pull of gravity, and it may eventually grind to a halt. At that point, the universe would begin to contract until billions of years in the future it completely collapsed in what some astronomers call the Big Crunch—the opposite of the Big Bang. All matter would disappear, and space and time would end.

The second possibility is that the universe would never stop expanding. Space would be boundless. Einstein's general theory of relativity would account for either possibility. In fact, according to the equations he developed, the universe can't be still. It has to be in constant motion.

Yet Einstein wanted to believe in a static universe, so he fudged his math and provided for a kind of energy that, in theory, acted as an antigravity force, pushing back against gravity's attraction to create a delicate and long-lasting **equilibrium**, the third possibility for the fate of the universe. As noted American physicist Brian Greene explains, "Einstein called this space-filling energy the cosmological constant, and he found that by finely adjusting its value, the repulsive gravity it produced would precisely

cancel the usual attractive gravity coming from stars and galaxies, yielding a static **cosmos**. He breathed a sigh of relief."

Einstein's relief may have come too soon. A few years later, Hubble's discovery that the universe was still expanding caused Einstein to revise his calculations to conform to Hubble's conclusions. Starting in the 1990s, two teams began studying the historical rate of expansion of the universe. One was the High-Z Supernova Search Team, an international group led by American **astrophysicist** Adam Riess and Australian astrophysicist Brian Schmidt. The other was the U.S. Department of Energy's Lawrence Berkeley National Laboratory, under the direction of American physicist Saul Perlmutter. The researchers thought they would find that the gravitational pull of all the matter in the universe—contained in its billions and billions of galaxies—would slow expansion

A star-forming region in the
Large Magellanic Cloud

Stephen Hawking has battled the degenerative disease ALS since the 1960s

SPACETIME ASIDES

(Mc)Flying to the Future

Perhaps the most successful time travel film in history was 1985's *Back to the Future* (followed by two sequels, in 1989 and 1990). *Back to the Future* begins early one morning when Marty McFly (played by Michael J. Fox) meets his friend, scientist Emmett "Doc" Brown (played by Christopher Lloyd). Doc Brown tells Marty he has invented a time machine, a plutonium-powered DeLorean DMC-12 that powers a device called a "flux capacitor." During the film, Marty goes both forward and backward in time. Noted American physicist Michio Kaku was asked to comment about the scientific accuracy of the film's time travel aspects. According to Kaku, going forward in time is the easy part. He points out that astronauts go forward in time by a fraction of a second because the faster a person goes, the more time slows down.

Going backward, however, is much harder. According to Einstein and the general theory of relativity, time is a river. With enough energy, this river can fork and create an alternate reality, as Doc Brown explains to Marty. "You jump from one stream to another stream," Kaku says. "*Back to the Future*, to my knowledge, is the only film which gets it right."

in a way similar to how a ball thrown in the air falls back to the earth.

However, the teams—both of which used data from the renowned Hubble Space Telescope—discovered that the universe was not slowing down, but continuing to expand at an ever-increasing speed. It was as if the ball kept rising, pushed by an invisible force. This unseen phenomenon, now called dark energy, carries its own set of mysteries. What exactly is it? How much of it is there? Will its strength vary over time? Riess's and Perlmutter's discovery of dark energy was just the beginning of their work. The two scientists shared the 2011 Einstein Medal, awarded annually by the Albert Einstein Society of Bern, Switzerland, and were encouraged to continue their surveys of the universe.

If the fate of the universe is the biggest question about space and time, how to time-travel is probably the most entertaining. As noted British theoretical physicist Stephen Hawking has said, "It is possible to create a time machine that will jump you forward in time. You step into the time machine, step out, and find that much more time has passed on the earth than has passed for you. We do not have the technology today to do this, but it is just a matter of engineering." One thing that makes time travel possible, at least in theory, is that people traveling nearly at the speed of light through the distant reaches of space would age more slowly than those on Earth.

A potential method of time travel involves something else that Einstein didn't like about his equations. Almost as soon as Einstein had published his general theory of relativity, a German physicist named Karl Schwarzschild showed that the theory allowed for the existence of phenomena later called black holes. These were the remnants of massive stars that had exploded. The remaining matter was under such intense gravitational pressure that a dot the size of a period would weigh hundreds of millions of tons. The pull of gravity was so strong that not even light could escape.

While no one has seen a black hole, other observations have led astronomers to believe that black holes are somewhat funnel-shaped. Some believe that passages called wormholes may link two black holes. Future space explorers might use these wormholes to avoid being crushed by gravity and emerge somewhere else many light years away. But even if wormholes exist, most calculations demonstrate that they would collapse almost immediately. Nothing could get through.

American physicist Kip Thorne disputes this finding, though. He says that a force similar to dark energy could push back against the crush of gravity and maintain the opening in a wormhole long enough for someone to pass through and perhaps even return. But this possibility exists only in theory.

Another theoretical possibility for time travel uses the curvature of space to reduce the amount of time to travel from Earth to distant stars. It would be the equivalent of walking across a large rug by first grabbing the far end of the rug and bending it back

Colliding galaxies such as the
Bullet cluster give scientists
information about dark matter

Eye in Space

The development of telescopes helped astronomers solve many of the mysteries of space. But their images were always distorted by Earth's atmosphere. The Hubble Space Telescope (HST) was an attempt to solve that problem. Named for pioneering American astronomer Edwin Hubble, the HST was launched into orbit around Earth in 1990. Right away a serious problem emerged. One of the telescope's mirrors had a slight imperfection. The error was less than 1/50th of the thickness of a sheet of paper, but it was enough to throw the images out of focus. Three years later, space shuttle astronauts corrected the situation. Since then, the HST has sent a wealth of information back to Earth. This information includes spectacular photographs that are much clearer than any available from Earth-bound observatories. Eventually the HST's components will begin to fail, and its usefulness will come to an end. At that point, it will be guided out of its orbit and crash into the ocean. Soon after that occurs, its successor, the James Webb Space Telescope (JWST), should be ready to launch into orbit nearly a million miles above the earth. This high orbit will allow the JWST to learn even more about conditions in outer space.

toward yourself. The distance between the two edges then becomes just a few inches, which you could span in a matter of seconds.

There may be other ways of traveling through space and reaching the stars. In theory, it is possible to travel at about 1/10th the speed of light, or 18,628 miles (29,979 km) per second, for sustained periods of time. This could involve aiming an intense laser beam toward a huge lightweight sail mounted on a spacecraft's exterior. In this situation, Jupiter would be a mere eight hours away. Travelers could reach Proxima Centauri in little more than 40 years. Small **prototype** sails have actually been tested in vacuum chambers at a fraction of the acceleration that would be required. The sails, however, are very delicate. Even a speck of space dust could cause serious damage.

In 2010, solar-sail technology moved beyond theory when the Japan Aerospace

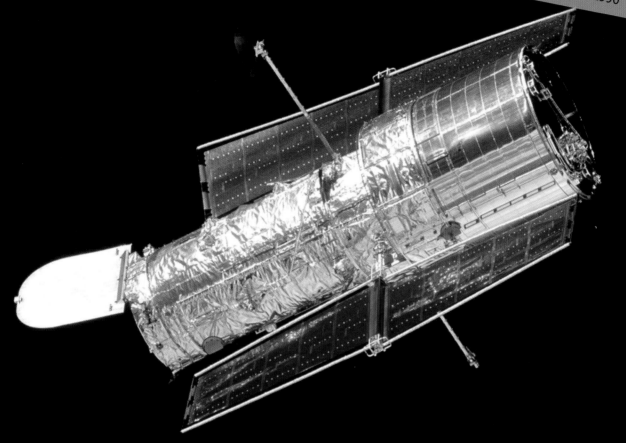

Exploration Agency (JAXA) launched its IKAROS (Interplanetary Kite-craft Accelerated by Radiation of the Sun) experimental satellite. Propelled by a 66-foot (20 m) solar sail and solar cells, the unmanned spacecraft flew by Venus and completed a number of inflight operations. JAXA anticipates building a larger (though still unmanned) version capable of journeying to Jupiter later this decade.

At some point in the future, humans will almost certainly venture far into space and unravel even more of its mysteries. As space becomes more defined and time becomes less so, we may even discover how both of them began—and how they may also come to an end. Or we may find that they are eternal and infinite. Only time will tell.

ENDNOTES

alkali metal — a soft, silvery, highly reactive metal never found in its purely elemental form in nature

astronomers — people engaged in the scientific study of planets, stars, and other celestial phenomena

astrophysicist — a person who studies the branch of astronomy that deals with the physical nature of the universe

atom — the smallest part of an element with the chemical properties of that element

Babylon — a city-state in present-day Iraq that originated more than 4,000 years ago; for a time, it was probably the world's largest city

cosmos — the universe seen as a whole

element — matter with a unique atomic makeup that cannot be reduced to a simpler substance

entity — something that has a real existence

equably — unvaryingly or steadily

equilibrium — a condition in which competing or opposite forces are in a state of balance

galaxy — a system of stars held together by mutual gravitational attraction and separated from similar systems by vast regions of space

geometry — mathematics of measurement, dealing with the properties and relationships of angles, lines, points, and solids

gravity — the force of attraction between all masses in the universe that causes objects to fall toward the center of the earth, and which keeps the moon in steady orbit around Earth and the planets in orbit around the sun

International Date Line — an imaginary line running from the North Pole to the South Pole largely through the Pacific Ocean; to its east, the date is one day earlier than it is to the west

intuitive — knowing instinctively rather than through conscious thought

Jack the Ripper — an unidentified serial killer who brutally murdered several young women in London in 1888 but was never caught

lunar — of or relating to the moon

nonspatial continuum — a continuous series having no width, length, or height

orbit — the curved path that a celestial object takes around a larger celestial object

parishioners — members of a certain church

pendulum clock — a timekeeping device driven by the regular back-and-forth motion of a pendulum; the most accurate clock from its invention in 1656 until the 1930s

physicist — a person who studies matter and motion through space and time in an effort to discover the physical laws of the universe

prototype — an original model of a new device that may serve as a basis for future products

vacuum — a space from which air has been removed

WEB SITES

Ask an Astrophysicist: Astronomy as a Profession
http://imagine.gsfc.nasa.gov/docs/ask_astro/profession.html
Find out how to become an astronomer or astrophysicist, and find new resources for further research.

Web Exhibits: Calendars through the Ages
http://www.webexhibits.org/calendars/moon-diy.html
Learn more about the history of calendars and track the phases of the moon to make your own calendar.

SELECTED BIBLIOGRAPHY

Baker, Joanne. *50 Physics Ideas You Really Need to Know.* London: Quercus Publishing, 2007.

Bryson, Bill. *A Short History of Practically Everything.* New York: Broadway Books, 2003.

Callender, Craig, and Ralph Edney. *Introducing Time.* London: Icon Books, 2001.

Davies, Paul. *About Time: Einstein's Unfinished Revolution.* New York: Simon and Schuster, 1995.

Greene, Brian. *The Fabric of the Cosmos.* New York: Alfred A. Knopf, 2004.

Hawking, Stephen, and Leonard Mlodinow. *A Briefer History of Time.* New York: Bantam Books, 2005.

Raymo, Chet. *Walking Zero: Discovering Cosmic Space and Time along the Prime Meridian.* New York: Walker and Company, 2006.

Wheeler, John Archibald. *A Journey into Gravity and Spacetime.* New York: Scientific American Library, 1990.

INDEX